DIAGRAM FOR THE CLASSIFICATION OF WORLD LIFE ZONES OR PLANT FORMATIONS

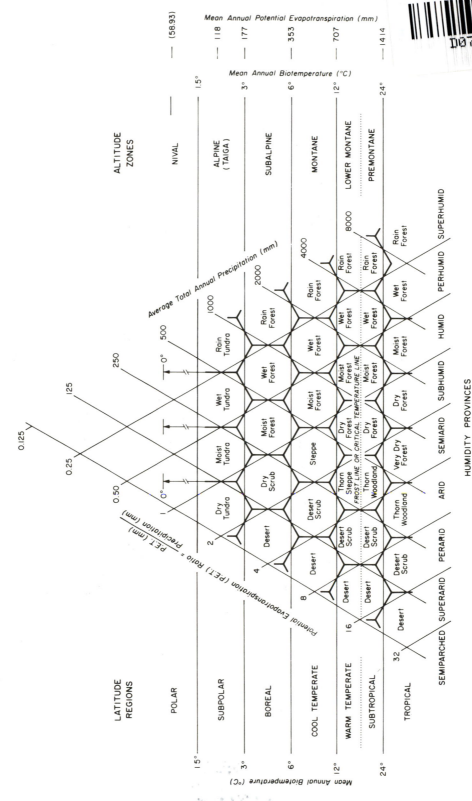

Redrawn from L. R. Holdridge, *Life Zone Ecology*, Tropical Science Center, San Jose, Costa Rica.

INTRODUCTION TO
Forest Ecosystem Science and Management
THIRD EDITION

RAYMOND A. YOUNG
RONALD L. GIESE

Editors

University of Wisconsin–Madison

WILEY

Acquisitions Editor	Keri Witman
Editorial Assistant	Maureen A. Powers
Marketing Manager	Kevin Molloy
Senior Production Editor	Sandra Dumas
Senior Designer	Kevin Murphy
Production Management Services	Argosy
Cover Photo	Old-growth in Memorial Grove, Cheguamegon National Forest, Wisconsin © Jeff Martin/JMAR Foto-Werks

This book was set in 10/12 Adobe Garamond by Argosy and printed and bound by Malloy Lithographing, Inc. The cover was printed by Phoenix Color Corp.

This book is printed on acid-free paper. ∞

To order books please call (800) 225-5945.

Young, Raymond A. and Giese, Ronald L., eds.
Introduction to Forest Ecosystem Science and Management, Third Edition
ISBN 0-471-33145-7

Printed in the United States of America

10 9 8 7 6 5 4 3 2 1